The Celestials

*With the Loving Guidance of the God Force,
the Universal Light, the Angelic Realm and
White Feather*

First Published in 2004

Revised and republished in 2009
Published in 2009 by:
Marie-Angéle Corynne Ormsby

© Copyright Marie-Angéle Corynne Ormsby 2009
www.whisperingsoftheheart.com.au

Printed by: KainosPrint.com.au
Cover Design & Production by: Naomi Baker,
www.intuitivecreative.com

ISBN: 978-0-646-50718-7

National Library of Australia Cataloguing-in-Publication entry

Author: Ormsby, Marie-Angéle Corynne, 1959-
Title: The Celestials / Marie-Angéle Corynne Ormsby
Edition: 2nd ed.
ISBN: 978-0-646-50718-7 (pbk.)
Subjects: Channeling (Spiritualism)
Dewey Number: 133.91

BOOK REVIEW by Simone Matthews - The Celestials

'The Celestials' is a book of truth, love and wisdom. It takes the reader on a celestial journey to discover that our purpose in life is simply twofold: to re-remember who we are and to self-love.

When we self-love and re-connect with our Divine Essence, we live in a blissful state of existence and create a Heaven here on Earth. Thank you Marie-Angéle for connecting with your authentic divine self, and bringing through these Universal teachings to help humanity BE LOVE.

I met Marie-Angéle at one of my Melbourne workshops (Essence of Angels), and was privileged to have been given a copy of her divinely channelled book. The book has been written with so much compassion, integrity and truth that I felt the need to share it with you all.

Simone Matthews
Metaphysical Teacher
www.universallifetools.com.au

BOOK REVIEW By Suzan - The Celestials

As a Spiritual Teacher, I try to engender within my Circles the ability to detach from the media's portrayal of life, to exercise wisdom, patience and unity whilst working within the Light leading to forgiveness, passion, peace and ultimately love. It was therefore refreshing to read "THE CELESTIALS" and find chapters dedicated within its pages, on how to embrace each of these important qualities. To me, the two most significant words Marie-Angéle has woven into this beautiful narrative are TRUTH and LOVE. Not seeing these as something we need to search or strive for, but showing us through her journey how she came to the realisation they resided within us all, no need to seek externally. In the same way, both whilst channeling and through Marie-Angéle's personal voyage of discovery, we are given the clear message not to look to the Heavens for God so creating a "separateness", but to feel the spark of His Love, Light and Presence within our hearts, our souls, our very essence.

We have all chosen to incarnate at this time and be part of the Earth's own Awakening causing new patterns of reality to emerge within our outer and inner worlds. The tender and gentle way Marie-Angéle allows us to venture into her own life experiences will indeed offer a guiding beacon to others travelling a similar road; the authentic voice to clarify many of the confused emotions that abound at this time. I therefore endorse this book as a tool for further Awakening to the Divine Truth and the Love we are all reminded to re-discover and embrace at this time. Marie-Angéle, THE CELESTIALS has indeed planted a seed of hope on the bookshelves and those that harvest this seed will join us in growing the ever-increasing Family of Universal Light hand-in-hand with our eternal friends in Spirit, the Celestials.

Suzan, Melbourne Spiritual Teacher, Channeler, Clairvoyant, Reiki/ Seichem Master www.wingsoflight.com.au

An Inspirational / Self-Help Book

To my wonderful children who bring simplicity, joy, warmth, love and humour into my life.

Thank you for all that we share.

"If I achieve nothing else in this world but plant a seed of hope in someone's heart, someone's life; then my work would have been accomplished."

Marie Angéle Corynne

In Honour of Thy Heavenly Father I dedicate this book.
That His Truth bear witness to our own Christ
Consciousness.

CONTENTS

INTRODUCTION

For only the Truth shall be spoken. Where there is Truth there is Life. God has spoken through my soul and asked that His Truth be shared with you. I am His humble servant and His work I shall endeavour to share with humanity.

We are all beacons of Light! Our God the omnipresent is the only Truth for there is no other. He is our torch; He is our rock. He is our inner strength and guiding force. He is the well of wisdom from which we drink, from which all thirst is quenched.

He asks us to look within ourselves and turn to each other to find Him. For there, the God spark lives. Looking up to the Heavens seeking this Truth only seeks to create a divide that keeps Him forever out of reach. We are created in His image and lives within us. Therefore He walks amongst us and does not reside above us.

For what He represents is our journey- the journey that leads to the remembrance of our own Divinity. He is our Creator - the Creator of all living things. Everything we hear, we smell, we taste, we feel and see is a reflection and reminder of our True Source. This is why He asks we look within and to each other in order to find Him. We are all a representation of His goodness.

The journey we walk is the journey in search of our selves
- our true selves.
The journey is about remembering Who We Are.
It is about embracing Who We Are.

The moment we separate ourselves from our own humanness is also the moment we separate from the Divine. We cannot be separate. Indeed this is our greatest challenge: remembering that we are all one, unified and that there is no 'better' or 'worse' in the human spirit. Spirit is pure. Spirit cannot be judged and trodden on or broken down. Spirit is our true self, our true essence. The journey is about remembering and embracing Who We Are.

God's invisible presence to the naked eye but fervent presence in my soul and my life has been my one and true inspiration. He has been instrumental in the orchestration of my life's unfolding journey. The search of my own life's purpose and mission; the search for inner peace and love, which defies the physical interpretation as we know it, has again and again unfailingly proven to me, the search begins inward. It has always and will always begin with ourselves and the journey similarly ends with ourselves, but without bondage.

The search for love has identified itself as the need for acceptance of the self and love of the self. Therefore my search for love has been the search for self-love, which is in fact my true essence - my Beingness. One cannot become what one already is! For indeed we are all kindred spirits temporarily clothed as we seek to echo our Truth, our Mission and our Divine Blue Print.

Therefore, there is no other purpose for this book but to spread Love, God's Love, to spread Awareness and to spread

Light. The Angelic Realm, and my guide, White Feather have helped make The Celestials a reality. They have given me the strength, inspiration and the vision. But more importantly, they helped me believe I could create this dream, which had been dormant for many years. They have guided me in the unfolding of my spiritual journey and in the connection of the reality of my true essence, a being of Light and Love.

Whilst channelling their words of wisdom, I have also revelled in the wonderful opportunity of evolving further on my own spiritual journey. They have helped me remember part of my life's purpose and part of my mission was not only in becoming more aware of my true self, but also to help others become aware of their true selves. I was being guided to see the bigger picture. As for helping others, I was unsure whether I could. More importantly, how I would do this? Was I adequately equipped in carrying out this work? It seemed such a huge responsibility. I was gently reminded however, that we are always given and come equipped with the tools necessary and appropriate for carrying out our mission.

It was at that moment I realised that all doubts and questions were coming from me. The lack of faith was not being directed from them towards me, but rather was within myself. Once I understood this, I instinctively knew it was my heart I had to open and allow to remain open to receive the guidance and support of the universe. They had patiently and vigilantly been waiting for my 'conscious awakening', my 'conscious realisation' that indeed We and the Universe are not separate.

It is only our belief based on how and what we think and feel which creates this illusion. The birth of my spiritual journey had taken place.

The dawning of my 'spiritual birthing process', my 'spiritual awakening', 'connection', 'realisation' or whatever one may wish to call it, had arrived at a time when inner turmoil and inner confusion were pretty much a part of my daily experiences. My life didn't seem or feel right anymore. I didn't feel right. There seemed to be gaps, which weren't there before. I felt like I'd been placed in a barrel full of debris and tipped upside down. From where I was sitting, there didn't appear to be any light, not even a very faint glimmer, and the climb upwards seemed and felt so far away and out of reach.

Looking around I didn't know where to begin. I was questioning my values, beliefs, likes and dislikes, many of which had been part of my life for some time. In short, I was questioning everything. My life seemed like a big question mark. What did I want to do? Where did I want to be? Why wasn't I happy in my job anymore? Why were the relationships with those I cherished, fraying and disintegrating before my eyes? Where did I fit in and belong? What was I doing here and where was my place on this earth? And the list went on. My head felt like a vortex spinning out of control.

The more I questioned the more frustrated I became, because it seemed at the time anyhow, that I was getting nowhere. I wanted answers there and then. I wanted answers fast. I wanted to get out of this mess. I didn't like the pain. I didn't like the confusion. I didn't like feeling numb. I wanted my old life back. It rapidly became crystal clear however; that no matter how hard I tried it wasn't going to happen that way. I relented to the obvious; that other plans were in store for me, so the search for new meaning began.

Whilst this search was taking place, I felt a strong and important need to review and pay attention to where I had been; the roads I had travelled, the experiences, friendships, relationships, jobs I'd had, and any other experiences which come along on one's unfolding journey. More importantly, I was questioning 'why' I had been on those travels and 'why' I had had those experiences! Were they somehow relevant to where I now stood and found myself? I wondered, was there a connection? Were they linked? Were they in their own right and of their own making going to help me, if I cared to pay enough attention, invested the time and was honest enough with myself to find out where I was going, and give me some answers to bring back into my life, some sort of order? I was having a mini-life review! Although not yet 'out of the barrel', I was feeling somewhat excited. There was anticipation at what I was going to discover. I began to warm to the idea of new possibilities, new opportunities, and a new life. Just the thought of something 'new' was exciting and refreshing.

So I invested the time, I searched, I reflected, I analysed and I was honest. As days slipped into weeks and months I noticed, slowly but surely, that finally I could see some light. The previous pain and confusion weren't as heavily loaded. There was a sense of aliveness. Life was taking on a different meaning, a different form and shape. This chrysalis (me) was slowly giving birth to its own beautiful creation. It was merely a matter of time before this butterfly would emerge from its cocoon - vibrant and full of new life, vitality and energy.

As time went by, I began to have a better understanding of my life's purpose, my place and my contribution. I began to truly understand myself. I began to better comprehend what the delicate, subtle and intricate experiences we face and encounter on a daily basis represented and offered. They were wonderful opportunities to better understand our selves and others. Indeed, those wonderful growth opportunities were blessings in disguise. It all depended on how we wished and decided to perceive them. Each experience magically woven into the next is not separate but relevant and relative, unveiling for us another piece of life's unfolding tapestry, the Web of Life!

My inner search, aided by the wonderful guidance of my gracious and loving companions helped to give me a better understanding of how and why we are all beings of Light and Love. After all, if I could not understand and believe this and see it as my own reflection, how could I truly and honestly see and believe this of others!

The Universe, I have come to understand, never imposes upon us and never forces us to do anything. It is always our choice, what we wish to do, where we wish to place ourselves, and what experiences we wish to have.

Personally, I had arrived at a point in my life where I wished to do new things, wished to be in different places, wished to have new experiences. I was ready for a new career.

I felt my days as a secretary were truly over. We had more than outgrown each other and it no longer brought me satisfaction and fulfilment. My inner being was crying out, begging to find new expression and to be set free. I felt stifled and suffocated, as if a part of me was rapidly dying. I desperately needed some time to think where my heart really wanted to be, but awareness of my commitments and responsibilities continued to keep me in the same line of work. All the while, I was growing unhappier to the point where my inner unhappiness was reflecting into other areas of my life.

Emotions of the physical body are the vehicles through which we traverse on our journey of self-discovery. Yet when calm and objectivity operate, we realise they are merely experiences belonging to the passage of time.

The turning point came when I 'accidentally' met a former colleague on my way to work. When he asked whether I was still doing the same job, my discontentment and lack of enthusiasm must have been blatantly obvious because he left me with these parting and echoing words: Then follow your heart and do what you love to do.

It wasn't until later on that day, the real impact of those words took effect. I'd have to honestly say, I have never held a job that I love. Secretarial work I had liked and enjoyed, but that's as far as it went. However, I did have a hobby which I loved, was my passion, and where my heart truly belonged. Writing! Writing had always been a part of me. It is in that space, I feel totally free to express myself. It is my centre where every part of my being feels connected and whole. It is the place where the me, who I am, truly comes alive. Sadly, like most of us I never seriously thought, or more importantly, believed that my hobby could become anything more than that. Of course, I had dreamt and fantasised, but as far as it becoming a reality, I guess I never really believed it possible.

A common misconception many of us have is thinking of our hobbies as simply hobbies. How unfortunate, as they may be our passports to a new life. So it was that after many rounds of debating 'Should I' or 'Shouldn't I', I finally acknowledged and surrendered. The time had arrived to take a leap of faith. And it was a momentous leap, because I was going into the unknown. But it was time to unleash this constant yearning deep within my soul to pass onto humanity, these words of hope, wisdom, inspiration and truth. It was time to honour those feelings. After all, hadn't the purpose of this soul-searching experience been to recognise and acknowledge who I am; to give my life its true meaning; to give my experiences a place where they truly belong and not appear or seem aimless and empty.

My search, upon reflection, has been one of the self. It has been an emotional challenge, which is at times one of the hardest. Nonetheless this also brings the greatest of rewards, and at times even the most unexpected of rewards to warmly and tenderly embrace. As with all things, it was time to reap what I had sown.

*The wondrous revelation of all is in realising
that we are all seeking the same sweet taste
of victory - Eternal Life!
It is already ours. It is merely a remembrance.
We are all aiming for the same destination regardless
of the many roads and turns we take.
Realising our own Christ Consciousness not above nor
below but alive within each one of us - The Ultimate.*

I now realise without doubt, the road I must take if I am to find and attain my own salvation. There is nothing clearer than that which stands gleaming and translucent as one looks at one's own reflection in the mirror of life. That upper and foremost is reclaiming my own freedom, attained when one seeks purely to work from and with the soul.

When we realise this Truth, we realise that it is from this level we must work to reach the Ultimate. We are not eternal upon this plane and once we accept this realisation and work within this concept then the physical things we give importance to will of their own accord, find their own order or simply disappear. Because we will "knowingly" replace them with things which move us forward and help us progress; thus expanding and inviting that which brings us closer to the circle of life.

We cannot hide from the Truth; the echo is too strong. Truth is for us to embrace and rejoice in. We must apply this Truth and indeed this is the challenge we face, for it is only through the application and the experience derived from such action, does Truth adhere itself to the soul imprinted forever.

I now know that I cannot turn back. Armed with this new awareness, this new sense of freedom and with the opportunity of discovering other parts of myself, there is a very strong desire not to remain static any longer. This awareness, pulsating to the beat of its own energy, infuses me with a new sense of purpose and wonderment and of looking at life in a totally different way. For you see, this is the real purpose of growth, it helps us to learn, reflect and move forward.

I have also come to understand how important it is to honour Who We Are: our thoughts, our feelings and what we were born to be. The most important thing we can ever do, the greatest gift we can ever give ourselves is to be true to ourselves. All of us are here for a purpose, for a mission. We all have our part to play. Once we understand and truly believe this, our lives will take on a different meaning. We will feel freer, happier and more contented. Our challenges will still be here, they will not simply disappear, but the way we approach them will be the difference. We will give ourselves the opportunity of not just seeing them on a surface level, but deeper, to the core within. We will find ourselves better equipped at detecting the opportunities those challenges bring to us, and how to turn them into growth opportunities.

Honouring ourselves will give us the opportunity of not walking aimlessly through life and simply going through the motions of living. We shall become more discerning of what we bring into our lives and where we place ourselves. We will want to be in situations that will bring expansion into our lives and into our hearts. When we do not honour who we are, we put on hold our birthright. Importantly, if we honour ourselves we will find others also honouring us because our lives will reflect and mirror that which we think and believe of ourselves.

*True freedom comes from the expression of one's
self - one's talents and ideas. It is that special touch,
shared and imparted with those who cross and share our
path and journey. It is the voice that speaks Our Truth.*

*True freedom is achieved by being in touch with our soul.
Nothing is more freeing to the soul than being what it
was destined to be. No one can take this precious gift
away but us.*

*Dare to open your heart. Shed all inhibitions and gently
walk through your fears, doubts and insecurities.
For there will you find your key.*

*True freedom is invigorating. It makes us climb
mountains, reach new heights, achieve the unthinkable.
It gives life a purpose. It brings us inner peace.*

This book therefore, is the by-product of my leap of faith. The words contained in The Celestials bear messages from the Universe, the Angelic Realm and my guide, White Feather. Their message is one of Love, to help us remember that this is the core of our being and to bring Peace through the Truths of which they speak.

They wish to spread Light so that the roads and journeys we traverse and the experiences we encounter can lead us closer to our purpose, our goals and our mission. They bring Awareness so that humanity may create a better world for all. They bring us Hope; they share with us their Truth and the beauty of their Wisdom. Most importantly, they help us remember our eternal link and that we are never alone, for their guiding force is forever vigilant and alive.

It has been an honour to have this opportunity of working together with my friends and companions. It's an experience I will cherish forever. As the writing progressed, it became obvious that the teachings they wished to impart were of the same nature I had longed to write about. We had the same intentions and goals. Our hearts were in the same place. We were working in unison. My friends and companions have a very strong desire to help humanity realise, recognise and remember its true essence. And the energy of their love and compassion for us all was always strongly imprinted in my heart. I sincerely hope that The Celestials resonates a truth within each one of you and touches your soul. I also hope it brings comfort, joy, revelations, warmth and peace. Most of all I hope you feel the love and passion within each word, for these were the instruments and guiding forces for this reality.

My companions, my friends have brought so much into my life, their guidance always through love and gentleness, and despite the many roads and challenges still awaiting me, having them by my side brings a deep sense of comfort, guidance and protection.

Let us always aspire towards the Light and let forgiveness, compassion and tolerance burn eternally in our hearts while reminding us, these are the underlying forces to the Love and Peace we all seek.

My friends, companions and I lovingly welcome and invite you to share and partake in this wondrous journey together. Open your hearts and feel our warm embrace, so you can echo your own truth in whatever experiences you encounter on your life's journey.

What is Truth?

Truth is the recognition of your own Divinity.

Never cease searching and seeking for truth, for your search and experiences bring you a step closer to your Eternal Home.

Peace and Blessings to you all.

Marie-Angéle Corynne

Your soul is a river that runs deep. Dare to delve into this vast wealth of knowledge, which goes beyond that of "human knowledge".

White Feather's Opening Message:

We welcome you, dear friends and are most happy to have you with us and to share in your company. The theme of this book is about love, simply about love and is the reason we have come to you and are here. We bring to you and humanity, truth, revelations and inspiration; these we bring and share with you and offer to you.

Our purpose is to pass on to each one of you the true essence of your beauty, the beauty of who and what you are, no matter what your station is in life, no matter what your colour or race, no matter what your standing in life may be. We come to you in peace. We come to you with love so that our love you feel may help you recall your own love within yourselves.

We ask and would like all of you, each and every one of you, to stop and look within where your true self lives; resides. We are here to help you rediscover and re-link with yourselves. We are here to help you remember Who You Are. It is purely a remembrance. All that you seek is within your grasp, with that we mean within your own grasp.

The experiences of the physical and the pleasures of the physical: We do not say not to enjoy, not to be grateful for these, for indeed they are part of your journey, part of your experiences, which make up the sum total of you, the all that is. But what we ask is that you learn to put these experiences, these niceties in their proper perspective. These are the gifts you take with you which adhere to your soul, we also ask that you assess for yourselves which of these are ever lasting, which of them speaks from within! And which of them will bring TRUE meaning to your lives? An example of how to do this is to ask: If everything MATERIAL was taken away from me, which of the things I PRESENTLY have in my life would I like to keep, to follow me wherever I go? Which of these has brought me GROWTH, which has brought me the most SINCERE gift, which has been the SIMPLEST gift?

For most of the time, it is in the simplest of gifts you shall find your jewel, your treasure, and WHICH EXPANDS YOU AS A TOTAL PERSON, AND WHICH REPRESENTS YOU FOR WHAT YOU TRULY STAND FOR.

These are some of the questions to ask your self. These are your truest tools, which you use to carve your path. These are the tools to add to others you have previously acquired, and learnt to recognise are worth keeping: tools, which will travel the distance and help you in becoming grandeur.

So my dear friends, we speak with so much love in our hearts. We speak with so much passion. We ask that you truly believe in us, in the wisdom we bring. We say this because we know what the journey is truly about. We are here merely to help guide you, to help you reconnect and to remember. We work with the God force, with the Heavenly Sphere in this purpose.

This is our mission, this is our purpose as we too, have also come to realise and recognise this truth for ourselves over many lifetimes. Now we are here to help you do the same. So it is a cycle. Cannot you see, that this is what the process is about, helping each other on the cycle, on the journey of life! Therefore, we are not here to misguide you. How can our love, a love so pure and genuine misguide you? If you ever doubt this, ever question this; then simply ask yourself the following:

Would love, a love clearly planted with good intentions, would this love truly misguide? And again, we would ask of you to reflect and remember, even if on only one incident in your life, when for a fraction of a second you found yourself resonate with the energy of love. A love that felt so right it left a mark, it made you think about it for days and left a feeling within you, which kept you thinking there was something different about it.

When this love resonates within you, inside of you, leaves its mark and urges you to want to find out more; more about where it came from, more of how you can experience it again and again; this is what we are about. This is the love we speak of; a love that truly guides you, and steers you in the right direction.

And so it is that in her personal search for discovery of the Truth, Little Feather is also helping transmit these messages to humanity. Her work is indeed a mission, a purpose. Her own experiences speak of their truth and what she transmits is what she has also been searching for. They are not merely words, but words that echo their own truths within her heart as it is with each one of you. Let your own experiences echo their truths within your hearts.

So my friends, we are here to share with humanity messages of love, messages of hope, to bring awareness, to bring hope and to bring peace. This message is from the Light, the words we speak, you may believe, as your very own as they resonate a chord within each and every soul, so you may all bear witness of the love that exists eternally.

Little Feather is my witness of the love existing between the heavenly spheres and the physical world. For my presence she feels, and she knows that this is indeed real, and could not be so if I did not exist. For the presence of my energy is felt as a living energy which is as real as your own, although of a different frequency, of a different vibration, of a different dimension not seen by your physical eyes but felt through your senses. For indeed this is not an extraordinary phenomenon to occur, but rather a natural thing, for we all co-exist within each other's energy. Only the level of your awareness separates you from this belief, from this truth. It is only time and your very own experiences, which will reveal all to you. As well, allow the messages contained within this book, and the truth within these pages guide you.

True service begins by acknowledging your
own identity.
It is being able to see yourself naked without fear
of the truth.

As you are all messengers in your own way, find out how you can be a messenger of truth. All of you have personal gifts and your own ways to be a messenger, for yourself and one another. Be a torchbearer for humanity. Be a torchbearer from within. For this Light forever burning within you will radiate outward in the world, illuminating the path for all those who follow. Such a grand spectacle to behold! It is indeed wondrous!

We see each and every one of you and we see nothing but beauty, basking in the vastness and the beauty of love itself, for there is nothing else. You see, you come from love and you come to the realisation that there is nothing else but love. The experiences you encounter in the physical realm, in the physical world, makes you realise with time, this very noble truth. Love is the completion.

Love is the sum total of Who You Are, of all existence. Love is the sum total of everything. This message of love cannot be spoken of too much. There can never be too much love, for each one of you brings his and her own energy of love in a different way to touch each others' souls in different ways, for indeed each one of you is unique.

Spirit, we ask that you do not forget about the Spirit. Spirit is eternal and it is for this reason we remind you that our love for you can never be severed. We are forever linked and forever bound in love and harmony. We live for eternity without judgment and without reproach. For once man sees with the eye of the Spirit then he will know and understand that this link cannot be anything but eternal. It is like a golden thread that penetrates between the two worlds, your world and our world. This golden thread is so very strong and firm. It is only your negative thoughts and emotions that can weaken the grip making it waiver from your end, but we are forever holding onto it, ever so tightly.

So my dear friends, these are our energies: LOVE ILLUMINATED BY THE BRIGHTEST LIGHT OF ALL, THE UNIVERSAL LIGHT THAT BURNS FOREVER AND SPEARS THROUGH ETERNITY.

We ask your permission that we may be able to place even a spark of this Light into your hearts, so that you can experience the difference and so you may give yourselves an opportunity of having this experience, of all. Always with gentleness, always with compassion is our intent, is our purpose - never by force. If you do not wish for this at this moment in time, if you feel you are not ready, we shall be waiting as we always are, for the moment when you are. We will take you by the hand and walk ever so gently, ever so softly beside you, whispering and sharing our words of wisdom; helping you open your own heart. We will rejoice with you as you rejoice in your own Divinity, in your own reflection that has mirrored itself within you for all of time and shall do so forever and ever. Your 'true' reflection is indeed the 'real' reflection of the person standing beside you, so 'see beyond seeing'. This is the true vision which helps you see and feel someone's pain, misery, hurt, happiness and joy.

The love of the Divine is all there is and it encompasses everything, including all religions. Love of the Divine, of the Great Creator is the pinnacle. It does not topple. There is no false hope or false illusions, for there is no illusion. There is only reality, clarity and truth.

So let not your religions separate and divide you. Each has a place for the teachings they intend or wish to impart. It is through respect of one another's respective affiliations that you will be able to appreciate and tolerate your different views, opinions and beliefs. Do not impose yourself on another, against their will, merely because you both don't see through the same lenses. For indeed, do you yourself not react when imposed upon, against your will? Do you always see through the same lenses as another? So we ask that you seek to see the commonality in each. Seek to see and understand what you are all searching for and indeed you will find common ground. How can there not be, when you are searching for the same thing, Eternal Life.

Let this common ground, let this commonality bring you together, harmonise and unite. For this is the fear you have in your hearts, that another will not accept you. This fear then keeps you separate. There is only one force, and that is the God force. You all come from the same source. Let this common ground, this commonality reduce your bloodshed, your tears, and your wars. Let the tears of blood run dry. Aim for tears of joy, tears of common ground, and tears of acknowledgment that indeed you are all one. Let this be in its stead, be in its place. Lessen your own suffering. Let there be no more bloodshed in your mind. Seek to find ways of bringing more unity. Listen. Communicate. Listen not with your ego but with your heart. One can only truly listen when one has removed fear from within. If fear is present, one cannot truly hear the words another speaks. Both cannot meet and truly communicate. Speak of your fears. If both of you have fears, then speak of your fears to each other instead of thinking, 'there stood someone before me who looked and appeared to be in control, but who had a presence I could not warm to'.

Let this 'presence' remind you, show you that this was only a front, a facade which had to be produced in order to protect, but their true being was another. Seek to see beyond. Lay down your arms, not so much in the artillery way, but the arms of defence you carry and take with you and harbour within you such as fear, pain, hostility, resentment, animosity, acrimony, hatred and so forth.

We shall always bring messages of hope, messages of love, and messages of peace. We shall always be here guiding you, helping you see your choices, your challenges and your life in more loving ways, firstly towards yourself and then towards others, for that is our only purpose.

Amen.

The moment you think yourself superior then at that very instant have you created your own separateness, your own isolation!
In order to be of service to others and to yourself, you must remember to topple false illusions of superiority. Spirit can only merge with Spirit - it cannot do so with the Ego.

The Angelic Realm's Opening Message:

We come to you in love. We come to you in peace. We ask that you surrender yourself to the God force. We ask that you give yourself permission to work more closely with the God force, with the Universal Realm and with the Universal Light. For there shall you find the peace that you seek, eternal and everlasting peace. For in everything you do in your daily lives, in your daily activities and underlying all you do and seek, is the search for peace and love.

You wish for your lives to be tinged with these vibrations, for these to be present. You are drawn to seek that which your very essence, the very core of your being knows is the truth, which indeed is those two energies we have just spoken of - Peace and Love. Furthermore, you will always gravitate towards truth and will always seek this when it is not present in your life because this is the true being that you are, your true essence. This is the reason you do not feel centred, do not feel balanced when these energies are not active and present in your lives. They are the energies, which you wish to operate in and from.

You all wish for others and yourselves to come together in love and peace. You do not wish for antagonism. It brings up your defences, so to speak. So we are here to remind you of the very being that you are, of your true nature. We are here to help you reclaim this; rediscover it. We are also here to help you find ways in which to have more of these energies in your daily lives, ways in which you can operate, and in which you can entice others to operate more from as well. Do not forget that at times we teach others by example.

You may wish others to be and act a certain way, but if they do not know how, then you can simply show them by being this yourself. They will be drawn to this example, for the soul will gravitate towards the truth. Our message is indeed very simple yet the experiences you encounter whilst on your journey may temporarily blind you, may temporarily make you forget that this is indeed what you are seeking, what you desire to have. So try and remember that which you are seeking when you are feeling out of balance and off centre. Stop and find a way to invite more peace and love into your lives.

We say to you that for the world to experience peace, it needs to learn more about tolerance, compassion and forgiveness. You all seek elsewhere, but we say and remind you that it is not where you believe it to be. It is all from within. People must be willing to look inward. It is such a simple task and we repeat this over and over, because it has not yet been properly understood, for more peaceful energy levels to be felt and experienced. We work with the Light, so we ask that you too, work with the Light through your heart centre.

We also ask that you look upon your disappointments, heartaches, losses, challenges and seeming obstacles as the gateway towards your spiritual journey. Give yourself permission to move through and beyond the adverse emotions and experiences you encounter. Be willing to be objective towards your own life for this will present you with the opportunity to see and understand the wider plan.

See beyond the physical vision.
See with your heart.
See with your soul.
This vision never dims,
never waivers.

Place your emotions, thought forms and experiences in their proper perspective. We will always be here giving you the strength, support and courage you may require and desire. Trust in the unseen who have and hold their own power, their own magic. Dare to believe above and beyond the tangibles in your life. When you truly begin to understand the real purpose behind the many challenges you face, you then gain the ability to move through and beyond those experiences. It is in that space where you can view and appreciate the true representation of your learning, and it is in that moment of acceptance without blame towards the self, another or the situation itself, can a shift take place in your consciousness, in your heart, taking you closer towards the unveiling of your own mask where Truth seeks to unite rather than divide and separate.

We say to you, putting situations and experiences in perspective brings you to the point of balance, but this requires honesty and objectivity. We ask that you learn to appreciate and accept all your emotions for they will teach you many things about yourself. For example, do you truly appreciate and savour an orange by only eating the flesh or only drinking the juice? The whole orange, each segment must be eaten in order to appreciate all the subtleties it offers: the flavour (bitter or sweet, tangy or juicy), the texture (soft, hard or dry) and so on. So must you do the same with your emotions and taste them all: their sweet taste of victory, their bitterness of hurt felt from the experiences you encounter or wrongful actions directed towards you by another. Do not discard any of them.

Be pensive without judgment, for this we say is often your downfall - judgment of the self and others. But you will learn, as you all must, that judgment cannot co-exist with acceptance. It does not lead to Peace. It does not lead to Love. It will result in a curdle effect and will leave you feeling somewhat uneasy. Do not make yourself wrong for an emotion. In order to learn the various shades it holds, you must first have the experience. Therefore, allow yourself to move through it. If you are not satisfied with the result it has brought you and taught you, then learn well from it so the same experience is not repeated; then remove it and toss it away without harbouring its energy like a long lost friend.

This wondrous gift is, not making yourself wrong for an emotion. We ask that you teach this well to your children, for this is the seed of guilt, which hides away your beauty, your diamond like sparkle. Do you not wish to sparkle? Do you not wish your children to dazzle in their own light, in their own brilliance? These are wondrous gifts. You are all doing so well on your journey. We simply ask that you be gentler on yourselves, more forgiving, for then will you also be towards another. Then will the energy on this planet grow finer and finer. It cannot do so through dense matter. It is too thick, too much like a fog, it cannot find its own way. Do not walk around in your own fog for too long because there is so much to do, so much to be claimed, so much to smile about, and so much to be shared. When you have given and allowed yourselves the time necessary to experience what you must, put on your 'perspective glasses' and view your life once again and notice what else you now see.

These things we have spoken of are the tools that will open the doorway to your own freedom, which you unfortunately tend to seek, expect and demand from the wrong places. Then the most wondrous things will happen. You will be a step closer to your mission and humanity a step closer to its own. Embrace and accept the opposite forces of your emotions, for they of their own making are also the point of balance. Embrace your Divine Spirit.

We understand your challenges, but you must see and come to comprehend the wider plan so as to integrate your experiences and learning, for they are not isolated from their own nature. All is forever linked.

For my children, we love you all so dearly.
With Peace and Love.

Amen.

Her presence I sense.
Her goodness I taste.
Her gentleness I feel.
For Mother Mary guides this wondrous place
we call Planet Earth.
Embrace it with love as She embraces you with
Her love infinitum.

LOVE

Love with the ferocity of your heartbeat.
Love with the gentleness and tenderness of You.
Love with the passion of your being.
Love with the river of your life force.
Love with the force of the thunder and lighting.
Love with the vastness of the valley
and the meadows.
Love with the awe of the spring budding flowers.
Love with the Great Creator in mind.
Love with the God force.
Love for love itself.
Love for the simplicity it holds.
Love for the forces it weaves and creates
in and for your life.
But most of all
LOVE FOR ALL MANKIND!

So there we are dear friends, our sharing of these simple but powerful words on Love we bring to you that you may reflect upon them, to see the divinity, the truth and the wonderment they can bring to your life, and the miracles they can create and manifest. These simple words we speak, we speak because we love, because we are, and because God is. And because You are the creature of God, the Great Divine Creator who has breathed life into your being, so that you may rejoice in the simplicity and beauty of You, and who You are.

Love is not the void you may feel when lacking the physical love you seek. Love is the spark that burns forever and so brightly in the depth of your being, permanently. It is the shooting star that manifests when you dare seek, and most of all when you dare to believe. For without belief, it is not possible for anything to exist or to be created. Love is not the darkness in the midst of your chaos. It is what you must give yourself when 'seemingly in your eyes' absent from your life or surroundings. So we ask you look at one another with love and compassion in your hearts. Not with contempt, remorse, regret, not with anger or with vengeance, for the way you look at one another is the mirror of your heart. Your brother and you are the same, are were created the same. There is no division in God's World, in God's Kingdom. There is only one force. The other emotions you experience, help you to understand its opposite force, for do you not always search for love, for peace? Do you not always gravitate towards love, towards peace? You do so for this is your very essence, your very nature - Who You Are. If you were all the other opposite emotions we have just spoken of, you would not seek and gravitate towards love and peace for the other emotions would be enough. But they are not enough, so there lays a piece of puzzle to the great mystery. Cannot you see that your souls, your hearts, hunger for love in all that you do, in all that you seek to be and to have? It is all tinged with the most beautiful energy of love and peace.

For indeed love colours life so beautifully. It adds a glow, a shine to everything else that may seem a little dull at present in your lives, for let us remind you that no matter what happens, no matter what situation you may all find yourselves in, love is always present.

Therefore dear friends, surrender to this truth, breathe it into your life and see what difference it can make. Give it a try, 'a shot' as you say in your world. Be daring! Try to live with this vibration even for a brief moment. Be conscious of it for a while, that is all we ask of you and see the differences it brings into your lives; see the responses of other people towards you and you towards them because the energy flow will be different, for love is magnetised by love - it cannot be repelled by it. Love brings people together, but if one is operating from love and the other from a lesser energy, then the two energies will not harmonise very well. Tension will be felt somewhere in the interaction.

We remind you that love can only equal to love and more love, as much as fear, hate, anger equals to more of the same.

So, which of these energies would you like to have more of in your life? Living with the energies of fear, hate, anger and other similar emotions will surely multiply themselves, for these energies are constantly being reproduced by your emotions, by your thoughts and so they grow and grow. So we ask, which of these energies would you like more of in your life, love; compassion; peace; tolerance; forgiveness? Even just one of these emotions existing at any given time in your life will make a change. It will add to your life a different shift, a different vibration and it will create a doorway, an opening for more of the same to follow which will in turn attract more similar emotions into your life. For you see, they are drawn towards each other, they are magnetised by each other, they are attracted to each other. And so it is that negative emotions operate in the same manner; the opposite forces in motion; the polarisation process so to speak. As a coin has two sides so does every emotion, every experience. All it is, is which side of the coin do you wish to operate from and in. But do not be too critical and hard on yourselves if you slip over to the other side of the coin every now and again, because such experiences remind you more of where you wish to be and remain; do not harbour them in your heart forever.

So many of you feel so hard done by, but we say and ask that you look into your own hearts first before you turn to your brother. See if there is anything you can change, you can alter even if a little before you turn to your brother and attack. For when one attacks another that in itself is a sign that he or she is hurting. Remember, one does not feel the need to attack unless one is feeling wounded, but attacking itself produces negative emotions, more negative emotions and so the cycle continues. There must be a meeting point where energies meet, where these energies fuse. You may not be able to change your brother's attitude towards you but you can change your own attitude towards yourself. Do not wait for another to do the changing.

Look around you.
Can you not feel your brother's pain echoing
in your heart?
Can you not see your joy in his smile?
Can you not see and feel his isolation reflected
in his gaze?
For my friends this is the Web of Life!

Begin with yourself and set the train in motion so to speak for by doing this you will be moving forward on the journey of life, taking your brother along with you if he so wishes, but if not, then taking others who are ready for a new experience and moving along. There are many others who wish to see the Light; who wish for their hearts to be illuminated, to be made light, to feel free, and to be shown another path from which they are presently on. If another has unfairly or unjustly hurt you, unfavourably looked upon you and you feel no recognition coming your way, then transmute your own pain if you must. Do not wait for others to do so with you, or for you, because they may not be able to or willing to at this point in their lives. Look within yourself and turn the experience around, remembering your own worth in the process. The key is to put it all in perspective, in its rightful place and to keep moving along.

Do not remain static in your own processes - by this we mean within your emotions and thought forms - for life itself is not static and will take you along with it, but it may not be where you would like to be, so move yourself along your own path.

Look around you. Everywhere you turn there is somebody who is in need of a helping hand, of love. Love has many disguises. It is shown and can be shown in many forms, in many ways: in a prayer, in a meal, in a handshake, in a gift, in a touch, in a word, in a gesture, in a smile. There are endless ways in which love can be shown, can be shared, and can be given. The love we speak of is the love of purity of essence that adds weight to your gesture, to your words, to your caresses, to your life itself. Open your eyes beyond your own back yard and look further afield to see who is in need of your love.

Love is such a powerful force it is to be shared, it is to be spread, and it is to be given freely. It is too powerful to be contained within one heart - this is the power of love. Each day, look around and see where you can spread your love. The opportunity will be there, this we can assure you. Everyday you can experience the beauty of love, to share it and to receive it. Open your heart to give it and open your heart to receive it. It is like filling the cup. As you empty your cup by giving, you replenish it again by receiving love into your life. It is a cycle that knows no end. It is a force that reaches into so many depths. It is a force that weaves itself in the most unimaginable of places. It is the force that brings life to your soul for were it not for love, what would you be living for? For are you not unhappy when love is absent from your life in whatever shape or form? Do you not feel despondent and empty? Love is the guiding force for all existence, for all creation, for all that is!

These are powerful words we share with you because they are important messages to comprehend; to understand; to believe; to feel and live. Yet, at the same time there is such simplicity in it.

Love, my children, spread the love that is in your heart.
Let it weave itself through your life.
Let love be your guiding force.
Let love be the spark that glides through your life.
Let love be the spark that burns eternally within.

PEACE

*How can you strive for peace in the world if and when you do
not have peace in your hearts?*
*For peace to be present externally it must first be present and
alive inwardly.*
*You must know how it feels to have peace in your hearts before
you know what to put out to the world.*
*Listen to me my children, how can you expect to have a
unified nation when you yourselves have an empty heart, full
of sadness, anger, resentment and contempt?*
*You must learn to lessen and banish these emotions for love,
compassion and humility to enter your hearts. Then shall
you know the true meaning of peace. Then will you be able to
experience a peaceful nation. First, find peace in yourselves
and with yourselves.*

*This, my children I say to you. This you can achieve only
through me, through loving me and serving me, which is
through my people. I walk among you everyday.*
I am everywhere in the Universe.
*You see me, smell me, hear me, touch me, and feel me every
passing minute of your day.*
*You scorn, hate, judge, resent and cast aside your fellow
beings every passing minute of your day.*
Remember, as you do these things the same you do unto me.
*Forget not that I truly exist in each and every one of you
so how can you not see me, smell me, hear me, touch me,
and feel me?*

FOR YOU MY CHILDREN -
MY LOVE IS ETERNAL!

Peace is found in the heart. Peace is found within. Peace is a state of being, as is contentment. Peace and contentment can be achieved by being in the presence of another, or in the surroundings of a particular place, but that passes, comes and goes. The peace we speak to you of is everlasting peace, one that resides within you and never leaves you. You may temporarily forget this when times are trying, when times are difficult, but it resides within and can be contacted, and called upon at any moment - even in those trying and difficult moments.

This is where you shall find the peace you are all seeking. It is an inner glow. It is an inner knowing that cannot be equalled. It is the surrendering to Who You Are. Peace my friends, is but a breath away. It can be attained in one lifetime, in your lifetime! The choice is yours. Ask yourselves; to what kind of peace you aspire? Do you desire to have in your lives, everlasting peace or temporary peace? Fleeting, in and out of your lives like the passing of the wind, the choice is yours and rests in your hands.

Experience has probably taught you that to anything and in anything there exists an opposite force, the positive and the negative. Therefore, it is for you to seek and find your own point of balance, to experience this for yourself. For when you achieve this point of balance, you will automatically feel at peace with yourself, your environment and your surroundings.

To find your own inner peace, we ask that you find the truth which echoes 'You', that speaks the 'You' that is. Do not be afraid if you do not have the same gifts, the same talents, the same lifestyle and possessions as your neighbour. You come equipped with your very own such things, designed to empower you on your journey and help you carry out your mission. You belong to you alone above all else; and this is the beauty in which you should relish. The passion, the care and the time that you invest into understanding another, we ask that you do the same for yourselves. Your own worthiness is also to be recognised.

So do not feel indifferent, or fear being ridiculed, because your neighbour and you do not act, think, feel or possess the same attributes or successes. You cannot and will not be the same. This is the law of the universe. You all desire to be and aspire to have a bit of this and a bit of that from different people. However, your own experiences, your own thoughts, your own feelings, and the talents you have brought with you belong to you alone and no one else; so how could you possibly expect to be his clone? So you see, what matters is in finding, acknowledging and treasuring the things that you possess. We say walk your own path. Be the master of your own life. Look for your brother along the way, but do not make less your own journey, do not diminish its importance because his 'appears' to be more important in your eyes. Everything has its place in the scheme of things and bears its own weight, its own purity and its own importance.

Do not compare. Sadly, this is what many of you do. You compare yourselves - your looks, your reactions, your thoughts, your feelings, your experiences and so forth - thinking more is better, that different is better. This is much like a cat chasing its own tail - the game never ends and you keep going round in circles! Remember dear ones, as much as you are capable of noticing and acknowledging what another possesses, know that you are also capable of doing the same for yourselves.

Find contentment in walking in your own shadow instead of another's. The beauty of seeing yourself for what you are for your own self-worth and the pressure of equating yourself to another is lessened, is removed, that in itself is worth its price in gold. This is the inner peace of which we speak.

Seek to surrender to your own Christ consciousness. Seek to surrender to what you came here to be and if you do not know what that is, then seek and search. The search itself can bring many wonderful revelations, many wonderful surprises along the way. Do not fear looking at yourself. The opportunities available to you are limitless, are infinite. Only your thought forms limit you and restrict you, nothing else. You create your own space in which you live in. You can choose to live in a big valley or you may wish to live in a shack. Expand your heart, open to receive. Your heart is either as wide as the valley or as small as the shack.

Surrender to the Light; let your heart centre be the shining beam spearing to the heavens. Let this be your eternal link. Let this be your source. Let this be our connection, for there we reside. Through your heart we speak to you. Feel our presence, feel what we bring and offer to you. Feel the serenity and the peace in the gifts we bring you and have to offer for they come with love, they come with a purpose. They come guiding your path, guiding your journey and your life to a better life, to a more joyful life, helping you find a different way of looking at life should the assistance be needed. We are here to guide. Speak to us dear friends; we hear your pleas, we hear your requests. Let gentleness enter your heart. Always allow gentleness to guide you, for gentleness carries further than harshness.

Peace be with you always and forever. Let loose the chains that surround your heart, let the shackles be removed. Be free. Allow yourselves to be free and to feel free. Invite us into your lives, and into your world where a new wealth of experiences await you. Let peace be one of the many things you seek, aspire to have and claim in your lives. Let it be at the forefront of your journey guiding you towards Truth, towards Knowledge, towards Wisdom. Let Peace and Love walk hand in hand for then you shall never be alone. They will be constant companions that never let you down, never fail you, but rather raise you to a new awareness, to a new consciousness and to a new vibration.

Inner peace equals freedom of the soul, equating to the discovery and the realisation of your true purpose and to your own victory as you find the real meaning of your very existence.

Peace is surrendering to the God force knowing all matters have been taken care of and that nothing has been overlooked.

Peace is realising that you are never separate, and never alone.

Peace is having the strength, having the courage of remaining open amidst chaos and pain.

Peace is walking hand in hand with the Universe. It is connecting with the God force.

Peace is unveiling the true being that you are to yourself.

Peace is surrendering to the knowledge that
you are a limitless being.

Peace is giving me, the God force, the opportunity of
working through you for there I reside.

PASSION

COMPASSION

Be still for a moment.
Observe, listen and reflect.
Isn't all human interaction, disguised in its myriads of
forms, based on the same intent - Acceptance?
You and your fellow beings mirror your own desires.
Ultimately Love conquers all.
This is the search.
This is the quest.
This is the truth.
This is the revelation.

Passion, Compassion. What do these mean to you? For love to exist in your hearts, in your lives, there must indeed also exist passion for life itself. So what is passion and what does it mean to have passion? Passion is the will and the desire to live God's Truth in your daily tasks and in your life. Passion is seemingly like drinking from the river of life. Life - magic, purpose and power. Life can be magical. It is all in your heart, dependent upon the passion you hold towards life. Like the river of life weaving its way up, down and around, so must you also be willing to reflect your life like the river.

Water is not fixed but fluid. So must you also be fluid; going with the flow of life and the experiences it brings to you; although in your eyes controversial at times, out of context and even out of time. But how are you to know that those experiences are not indeed leading you to your next destination, where peace and beauty await you.

Wishing to remain static and immovable does not allow the river of life to take you along its journey. It must swim around you, as you stand there motionless. So life can glide before your very eyes, taking along with it many wonderful opportunities and experiences. Be vigilant and watchful over your own life! Have the desire to want to live your life to the fullest. Have passion towards life, otherwise it is your own life you put on hold. Have the desire to discover your own magnitude. Metaphorically speaking, allow us to give you the following analogy: Imagine yourself and your life as an onion. With each layer you peel, more of you, what you are about, and of your life is revealed. As you discover more, allow this discovery to entice you to go deeper and to look further, for as you laboriously and carefully apply yourself to your task, it is only through such application and your industrious efforts that you will find yourself nearing the core. Furthermore, the many turns you will take on such a journey will give you the opportunity of becoming more compassionate towards yourself. Because you do not yet know what your own experiences and discoveries hold, until the next layer is peeled.

Those experiences and discoveries are the tools towards the softening of your own heart. When you learn to introduce dignity, humility, integrity and compassion in your own life and live within its principles, then indeed you will find yourselves better equipped in having passion and compassion for life itself. This knowledge and wisdom you can then apply towards other people.

So we say, have compassion for your sister, brother and yourself, for love cannot exist by itself. It needs other ingredients to combine with. Love is the base ingredient and the other ingredients help to keep love alive, to make love grow. The other ingredients awaken love, the love that already exists in your hearts, in your souls, in your lives. They are the sparks, so to speak, shall we say. Therefore, tolerance, forgiveness and humility are also important ingredients to incorporate.

Your heart knows when it sees the truth, when it hears the truth and when it speaks the truth. It is drawn to it like a magnet. It feeds on it and brings new energy to you and makes you feel alive inside. It makes you feel anew in your hearts and in your souls. So we say, and stress the importance of looking in your own hearts to find all of these ingredients. Bake your own cake with your very own ingredients. All of you bake your own cakes then bring it to each other as an offering to be shared. Taste all the wonderful flavours it contains for all of you will bring a cake yes, but it will be embellished differently. It will have a different flavour, a different texture, a different lightness, and a different colour. All of these differences indeed making up the different qualities that you all bring. All tinged with the same basic ingredients, but all baked with your own individualities, each imparting something special to each other by the sharing of your cakes. It is wonderful. It is indeed magnificent to know and to see how many cakes there can be. Each one glowing with its own vibration, with its own energy but baked with the main ingredient in mind, with the same motivating factor, and that is Love. Indeed we revel in this beauty. It is so wondrous in our heavenly spheres. You could not imagine the brilliance, the radiance of your offerings, of your gifts that you all bring. All so simple but so powerful, so grand and this brilliance, your own brilliance, can shine in your own planet, in your own sphere. It is possible. It is alive in each and every one of you.

All we ask is that you simply look within and see another in yourselves. The thread is forever linked. This is the web of life. It is a link that never ends, that never severs. Only your thoughts sever it, in your mindset, but not in your true reality, which is pure essence, and already exists and can never, ever die. All that is needed is an awakening of your own hearts, a vision, to see this wonderful truth. However, there is no hurry if you do not wish this to be so at this present moment for we know, you will all get to this destination point in your own time, for indeed this is the destination for all of you - the recognition of yourselves for the true beings that you are, embellished with the wonderful energy of love that spears through anything and everything that you could possibly imagine. This is the wonderful energy of love. It has the power to turn anything around, to make clean, to renew.

So we ask that you ponder on these wonderful thoughts, we bring and share with you today. All of you are beautiful beings. Is it not wonderful to know, you are already this being? You do not have to go and seek these emotions, these feelings, and these ingredients. All you have to do is awaken them and they simply come alive, as if awakening from a long sleep. Then simply watch them grow into this wondrous being that you are, into this wondrous light emanating from your heart centre. Look at them spear through to the heavenly spheres - your connecting link - and watch magic happen in your life.

So it is that we say to you dear ones, having compassion for one another is the force that will draw you together. Allow yourselves to imagine what it would be like to experience someone's pain, someone's hurt, someone's sadness, even joy and happiness. Try to imagine this hurt without wallowing in pity for them. Imagine their joy without envy, for that is indeed different, that is the lower energy. Instead, look to your brother with compassion in your heart, with love in your heart asking yourself what you can do to lessen and alleviate his pain for this will help encompass and fuse your energies where a division does not exist but rather unity through the seeking of understanding.

Surrender to the limitless being that you are.

LIGHT

Let the Light shine through your heart my brethren. Place your burdens, your sorrows, and your pain into my hands. No words need be spoken for all is understood.

Be in the moment. It is so important to try and be in the moment, for what it brings, for what it is NOW; for tomorrow brings itself to you. You do not have to make it happen, it already happens of its own accord. But what it brings to you in your tomorrow, is what you have allowed yourselves to experience in this now moment, this is the difference, and this is the key. It is so important to be and live in the now while seeing what you have, for my children indeed you have so many wondrous things happening in the now moment. Simply open your eyes and look around. Look inside of you and simply watch it grow and watch it happen. Anything, you want to be, can be.

We realise, at times you do not believe this and even find it hard to believe; that anything you want to happen can happen! But indeed this is a true reality, for do not your negative emotions bring you more pain, more negative realities? So why should not your positive emotions, your positive thoughts bring you positive realities as well? We are here to help you realise this. We are also here to guide you through your painful moments, through your dark hours when you feel most alone, as if no one in this world could possibly understand you, comprehend you. We ask you to simply tap into your heart centre and call on us. It is that simple. Just whisper our names, my name, it matters not. Call on the Universal Light and our help shall be given. Our help will spear down on you quicker than lighting for it is instantaneous. But first you must simply leave your heart open, for with a closed heart our help will simply bounce back to us, and there we remain unable to help you and guide you, to bring our peace, to bring you our love for indeed we love you all so very much. Watch our love spear through your life and watch it clear away all debris, all negative emotions. That is all we bring to you because indeed this is what we are, pure love; all that exists in our plane in its purest of essence. It feeds us. It is the well from which we drink. It has been given to us by God our Heavenly Father whom we adore, whom we aspire to, whom we fervently have in our hearts, always and forever.

So we bring to you this message of hope, this message of reality that you may come to realise and believe, the Father is indeed in you. The love, which the Father has given, is indeed for all of you, each and every one of you. Not only for a few. It is indeed the same, equal. Not more for some and less for others. It is your belief in yourselves, which makes you think one is more loved than the other, but in God's Kingdom there is no such thing. He loves all equally. All are loved with the same force, with the same gentleness, with the same compassion, with the same intensity. It is merely your experiences here on this earth plane that makes you believe otherwise.

But we say to you and remind you, that it is not so. Again we ask you. Look inside yourselves to recognise this truth, this simple truth, for the Father patiently waits until you come to this realisation. There is no pointing of the finger so to speak. There simply is, waiting until you come to recognise your own being ness, your own Light, your own divinity, and as each one of you comes to this realisation you light the way for others to see their own divinity, their own Light. You are like Light bearers guiding the way for each other. As one being is illuminated, the path is illuminated for another coming behind so that he may see his path with more clarity.

Think of yourselves not as dense matter or form but merely as vehicles of Light gently moving amongst one another's aura and energy field, gently connecting with the Universal Light and drawing into your life this vast and immense source of knowledge and wisdom. See yourself as a Being of Light connected with the Source and see unfold before you miracles that know no end.

It is indeed a wondrous sight from our heavenly spheres. You are like torches each leading one another forever forward. Isn't wonderful that it is always forward that you lead each other.

Once you see with your 'true' eyes, your 'true' vision, you realise this is the only way to move - forward, climbing the mountain and going upwards. Climbing on your journey and aspiring towards your true 'beingness' until you reach the peak of the mountain, and then you look down and you see love all around you.

You are surrounded and supported by love and with love, and as you see your brothers and sisters on their climb, on their journey to love, you know in that moment in time, in that very instant that it is all right, that all is well. Compassion then oozes from you, from your heart centre and you give it, you pour it out helping your brothers and sisters on their journey, on their climb because some may find the climb a little more difficult than others.

This is how it is. Masses of Light beings, torches already illuminated from within, waiting to be radiated outwardly. Indeed it is most wondrous. We would like so much for all of you to see your truths, to see your own beauty. It means so much that you find your own journey towards the Light because we hold you all in such high esteem, with such high regard in our hearts. You are all precious jewels, sparkling like diamonds. We revel in this wondrous beauty, and we pass on to you; we share this truth with you today that you may go and tap into your own energies and be Light bearers to one another and for each other. Help your brother and sister along their journey and they will help you on yours. What you do not see in yourself, another will come on your path and share with you and you in turn will do the same for another, and forward you will all move.

You may ask, 'but doesn't the journey begin inward?' We say yes, it begins inward but the difference is, it does not stay inward, it is shared, for once the revelation of your true state is found, it brings such joy you will want to share it with others. Because of the intensity of the love you will experience, you will not be able to contain it within yourselves and more than that, you will not want to. It will be that powerful, that strong and that is the purpose of it. This is how the illumination process takes place. It has to have a beginning point but then it is spread forward, around you and behind you, to be moved along the path, along the journey with a clearer vision.

But for those who feel they cannot move forward in that moment in time, cannot see or understand what you have to share with them, do not trouble yourself for another will come his way at another stage and shine the Light. There is always Light around you, always. You are never without it. It is only in your mind darkness is created, not in your true state, not in your true being, not in your true reality. So it is that another will come along, and when the time is right for a person to be awakened, they will be taken gently along the journey, joining with their brothers and sisters. In turn they will awaken another behind them. As you can see, you are all doing this work together. This is why we say you are never alone. We send you angels to enlighten you, to guide you. We send you beings to guide you, as we are also here guiding you. So together, with the forces combined, we feel we cannot go wrong.

It is all a matter of time. The Light shines from above and the Light shines amongst you. There is Light everywhere. Let your own heart radiate and shine this Light. We stand here guiding you with love in our hearts that you may experience it in your own hearts, that you may believe this is possible, for indeed it truly is. We only share the truth with you for this is what we are - beings who bring truth to the human spirit, beings from the God Source who speak the Truth of God.

So be a Light bearer and shine the path. Shine the way for others. Let your heart beam like a torch and let it bring more clarity into your life, onto your path and watch it branch further afield. Watch the Light spread and shine a broader span for seeing. The physical eyes can at times seem only to be looking through a tunnel, much like having tunnel vision. However, when you allow your heart to shine and bring through its guiding force, then all of a sudden the tunnel is expanded and you can see from all directions, it reaches further into the distance. For you see dear friends, looking through, and with a tunnel vision is very limiting because the darkness existing within the confines of this tunnel cannot and does not spread very far. It makes things look very restricted, very square box like, but that same vision can be made to look different if you so wish and desire.

The intent always comes from you, from what you want. So ask yourselves, what do you want, to walk in darkness or to walk in the light? We say to you, even if you have been walking in and through tunnel vision for a while, or even for a long time, it doesn't matter for time is irrelevant. You can change all of this in an instant just by your desire, just by your intent. It can all happen. Everything is possible! Through the energies you bring with your intention, you create a new reality. From this new reality, you draw new energies to you, bringing to you another reality and so the cycle continues. You see, with each new reality you create, there also exists energy in motion. You feed your realities with your thoughts, with your emotions, with your desires. Remember, there are two sides to the coin, for all of you have experienced darkness in your lives have you not?

So we ask that you allow yourselves the experience of 'having a go' at walking with the Light, and in the Light for even just a brief moment. Just allow yourselves the chance to experience something different, something new. Allow yourselves the opportunity to see and live from a different angle, from a different perspective. All it takes is a simple but strong intention and desire; then set yourselves in motion for the experiences it will bring. We can assure you, you will not be disappointed for the Light never disappoints. Instead, the Light will make your daily events, experiences and challenges 'lighter'. It will not make you feel so weighed down, so heavy. The Light uplifts, perks you up and brings a spring to your step.

Hope is the torch that burns brightly in the night and leads us when all else seems lost.
Hope is that inspiration that moves us closer towards our destination.
Hope is survival.
Hope - a ripple that knows no end in the vast ocean of life.

WISDOM

Wisdom is power transformed and operating from its higher vibration.

Wisdom is following your inner guidance from experiences learnt in the past. It is putting together these experiences and applying the wisdom you have attained from them in your present life, so that you may guide yourself and others you touch. But first you must avail yourself to the experiences coming across your path. Look at what they may teach you. Look with your soul.

You see my friends, you may hold a leaf in your hand and think nothing of it, but this leaf may teach you many things; it may be a clue to the tree it belongs to, it may tell you something about the nature of the tree, the fruit it bears (if any), its lifespan, whether the tree is in good health, what other vegetation may surround it and so on. It may appear to be a simple leaf, but the knowledge it holds and contains is so much more, and the next time you see a leaf of the same kind you will remember what it has taught you previously.

And so it is the same with experiences. Remember what they teach you and have taught you. Look for the messages - what you could possibly be deriving from having them, from being in them, and then learn from them. Above all, learn well. Be discriminating towards the experiences you come across, then armed with this wisdom you may walk more clearly on your path, able to guide others from those experiences, others who may be walking a similar path to you. Wisdom is the truth being spoken to you from your soul. What tools do you use for your journey, those carved by others or those carved by yourself?

Be wise in your teaching; be wise in your learning. We say to you, using wisdom in your lives makes the road clearer and gives you opportunities, new learning and new experiences. You cannot move to the next step, to the next rank until you have mastered your present status. It is much like going to school - you cannot move to the next grade unless you have mastered the teachings of the present one, because you will not be able to fully appreciate or understand the new teachings and experiences the next grade has to offer. So be vigilant in your own lives.

Wisdom is also being true to yourselves. It is walking your own path proudly. It is walking in your own footsteps and not in the footsteps of another. It is respecting another enough not to encroach upon his path. Wisdom is also knowing how much of yourself, of your energies you need to give to situations, because if you give to the point where you are exerting more than your being can cope with, you will feel depleted and out of balance. This is a fine art but one which can be learnt through observation and by listening with all of your senses. Wisdom is at times even removing yourself from a painful situation, so that another may learn a lesson. Being at their side to guide and to help, but not to overtake and interfere. This may be and can at times be a hard lesson for you to understand and put into practice when you feel much pain in your heart at seeing someone you love and care about or someone else around you suffering. But this is how wisdom will be adhered to his soul; from the experiences and lessons he walks and traverses.

This is why we say to you learn well, so as to minimise the pain in your own lives. You are your own wisest teacher and know what is best for you, more than anybody else. You know exactly what is right for you - to the exact degree - if you care enough, if you are brave enough to be honest with yourself. Others may come close, but they will never know exactly what or how you feel and think. They may be able to sympathise with you and even give you comfort from their understanding of similar experiences they may have had at some stage in their lives, but they will not be able to mirror your soul.

Wisdom is having learnt from your experiences, and the lessons which you were meant to have. It matters not in what condition; in what situation those experiences may have been encountered. What matters is how well you have learnt from them; in what way it has carved your character; in what way it has pushed you further along on your path, and how much more it has helped you understand yourself and others.

Wisdom is how much more depth you can bring to a situation, to an emotion; how much further, how much broader you can see, and how much more light you are able to shed on a situation. It is how much kinder you can be to yourself. It is also giving yourself permission to make mistakes, knowing that you must indeed be in certain situations in order to learn from them, that knowledge is acquired from being in the experience. Therefore, wisdom is also displaying kindness towards yourself and another. It is knowing when to remove yourself from a situation, which is not serving you for your highest good, and for your learning that will take you further along your spiritual journey.

Wisdom is knowing when to bow gracefully, recognising and accepting that you have done and given your very best; acknowledging that you have learnt everything possible, giving yourself permission and the opportunity of being placed in a better, higher position in order to learn more, in order to be expanded further, so as to see with a broader vision, and with a more open heart.

Listen with your heart and not just your ears.
See with your heart and not only with your eyes.
Think of where your heart wishes you to be.
Feel your reality.
Only you know where you wish to be. Take an
active part in the making and in the unfolding of your
own life. Do not allow yourself to follow blindly without
first questioning your own path.

Wisdom is allowing yourself to be expanded. It is, understanding the principle behind life, which is pure expansion through the vibration of love, through the vibration of goodness, of compassion, of tolerance and of forgiveness.

Wisdom is not equated to shrinkage, to contraction, which only serves to remove you from present or further experiences you may come across in order for learning. It is not about shutting yourself away, because the pain is too much to bear. Instead, it is bringing kindness to yourself in the midst of that emotion, of that pain and seeing what lessons you are learning; what gifts it is bringing and has brought you. For those very experiences could be the doorway, which sets you free.

Now isn't this a feeling of expansion, FREEDOM - FREEDOM OF THE SOUL, allowing itself to be where it next desires to be, in order to grow more, in order to find more joy, more harmony, more peace, more contentment. Is this not wisdom well learnt, well mastered?

It takes great courage and inner strength to remain with that focus in mind when a situation is not going your way, or in the direction you may have wished. But we say, and we ask, that you gently stop in your tracks and reflect upon the situation and look at all the angles possible.

Do not bring shame or blame into your thinking and into the equation, for shame and blame are not and should not be part of your reality. Acceptance of the self cannot co-exist along side shame, along side blame. These will only serve to remove you and stop you from looking deeper because they will make you feel 'bad' in your terms, in your terminology.

However, we say there is no bad, there is only a different way of looking at things. You are the ones who have given yourself this terminology of 'bad', but it is negative and only serves to isolate you from yourself. It makes you disown yourself because you do not like what you feel, and you then say you are ashamed. Be kind, be patient, be tolerant towards yourself and acknowledge, if you must, your position, your action and LEARN WELL FROM IT. This is the difference. This is wisdom. It is so sweet the taste of victory, mastering yourself. Be kind in your faltering, and if you find yourselves having the same experience again and again, one that you had hoped not to be repeating, stop and look at what you are perhaps not paying attention to, or not wishing to look at honestly. Look at what is holding you back, what is removing you from being able to surmount this repeated experience which is, of its own making, holding you back along your path and creating more pain for yourself in the meantime.

Wisdom is honouring and acknowledging yourself for the beauty and the jewel that you are. Wisdom is glory combined with the God force and with the love of the God force. It is beauty, it is harmony but most of all it is peace. It is bowing in recognition at the experiences your higher self wishes you to have and not the experiences your ego wishes you to have. Reflect and analyse from what level you are operating. The ego will separate you from the truth you already have and know. Tap into the wisdom of your soul and there all shall be revealed to you. Your soul knows what it needs in order to grow, so this is the very reason we gently say to you, with kindness and compassion in our hearts - stop and reflect and listen to what your body is telling you. You are always guided with feelings and thoughts. Reflect and discern from what level they are coming. Are they from your ego or from your soul? Does your entire body speak to you? Learn to recognise your own signals because only you will know how your soul speaks to you. Everyone is different. Each one of you resonates differently, but all of you will have one thing, one element in common, and that is with all of you, your soul will always speak to you.

Perhaps you may feel some anguish, some sorrow at having to make a decision, letting go of a particular job, a particular relationship, severing a friendship, or the letting go of anything. But if it is your soul speaking to you, who are you to question that something better is not on its way, although you may not yet see it, and know in what form or shape it may come, because it is not yet tangible.

However, you can feel reluctant to let go of what you own and have. Encourage yourselves to have faith and trust. The universe and you are combined and work in harmony. This interaction is always being conducted whether or not you wish to believe, and avail yourself of this truth. Certainly a lack of faith we must say, makes it a little harder for you to hear us and to notice the part we play in the unfoldment of your life.

Gently try to understand the nature of your soul. Try to understand its true purpose, its true mission and its intention, which is to aspire further towards the Light; towards your own truth, which is the Father, the God force, the Universe and Yourself, all combined:- AS ONE, UNIFIED; NOT SEPARATE BUT AS ONE, FOREVER AND EVER.

The truth and the beauty of the words we have just shared with you speak for themselves and we simply remind you to be honest, tolerant and kind with yourselves for this is the only way to move along the path. Being harsh, hard, uncompromising and unforgiving will not help you towards this task. It will blind you. We see, hear and understand more than you think, but vigilant we remain whilst the experiences you must yourselves traverse in order for the knowledge to be acquired and given the opportunity of being transformed into wisdom, which is then adhered firmly to your soul. Listen to the words we share with you, for all is given in the name of love. We love you all with high regard, with high esteem.

We love you all with our highest of compassion and for all living things combined. We Love you for the 'You', for the 'We' and for the 'Us' that We are, as One - Unified.

Amen!

Your thoughts travel through time and space.
They hold a powerful force that manifest their
own reality.
So participate in its creation for it will surely come back
to you as you placed it to the universe.
Be responsible for your own creation.

PATIENCE

Patience is, understanding another as you would like another to understand you.

Patience - what is patience? Ask yourselves this question. Ponder on it a little. Reflect, look within and find its true meaning. Patience we say to you, is firstly being kind with yourselves when you do not appear to understand something on your path, which has been presented to you for your learning, for your growth.

Patience is searching for answers, for understanding whilst you aim to understand yourself and another a little better and a little further in the process. It is allowing for the correct experience to take place and not rushing things to happen before their time. Rushing, making or wishing experiences to be hastened only produces and brings half-hatched results with only half the lessons learnt, which is then a waste of time and energy.

Patience is allowing seeming obstacles to unveil and unravel themselves to you; and to offer to you their blessings disguised in the experiences they bring. It is allowing yourself to walk the path, allowing and giving yourself permission to be led to the right destination, to the right clues, which will give you the missing piece or pieces to your puzzle, to your mystery. Patience is having the courage to walk a particular path even when at times you are uncertain which direction to go towards; feeling as if you are blindfolded, but still having this inner knowing, having this faith that you are being led in the right direction where things will unravel themselves to you in their own time. It is not forcing answers to questions. It is not making situations happen a certain way because you cannot or do not appear to be getting anywhere. Patience is asking of yourself what you must first do in a situation before asking the same of another. Patience is taking the time to be still.

For this we say to you. How can you be patient with another if you are not patient with yourself? Again it begins with the self. You will discover and realise along your journey that all begins with the self. How can you understand the true meaning of patience if you have not experienced this yourself in its proper manifestation? True patience is, symbolically speaking, walking along with your obstacle, with your dilemma. It is not running through it because the pain, the uncertainty is too great to bear, too painful to carry, and because of this, wanting to get to your destination quickly, so as to shorten and minimise the pain and the emotions you may be carrying and experiencing. Running through your obstacle or dilemma may help you get to your destination quicker, but what would you have learnt along the way? What would you have noticed, observed and reflected on along the way? What would you have appreciated? What light could have been shed on your behalf? Taking your time may help you avoid more pain in the future should another similar situation present itself to you.

Therefore, patience is giving permission for growth to take place within its own time frame. It is also understanding another in a different way and seeing another from a different angle, which you were unable to do previously. It is by its own merit, also giving permission and the opportunity for another to understand you in a different way. It is allowing the fruit to ripen in its own time. Patience brings compassion towards yourself and another, giving you a broader vision of yourself and of situations. Patience is basically giving whatever situation you find yourselves in, the opportunity to deliver and to bring the results it was destined to bring. Interfering with the process does not give permission for the teachings to be brought to you while also offering you many new gifts in its wake.

So we say, you cannot ripen something that is not yet ready to be ripened. It is all within its own time frame. We remind you to appreciate what you presently have, because looking at and focusing on what you do not have, asking yourselves why it isn't there and why it hasn't happened, makes you miss out on what is happening at the present moment. You blind yourselves to what you presently have, and you do not allow it, you do not give it the opportunity for growth. You cut the process short. You want the finished product without having given a chance for the beginning and the middle process to take place and to merge, which in turn will lead to the finished product.

Be patient. Remember that you are all learning through your experiences, and if some of those experiences you would rather be without, then seek to find their purpose. Perhaps you are learning more self-love through a painful process. Perhaps it is helping you realise that you are more deserving of love and are worthy to have more of it in your life, and a particular experience is not providing you with this. But by taking the time to reflect, you realise that it has taught you something about yourself. It has awakened something in you and then the decision is yours as to what action you wish to take, but first allow yourself the opportunity to learn from it.

We cannot remove you from any situation. We can guide you, make you see things from a different perspective but we cannot do it for you. It is all part of your own self-recognition, part of realising your own worth. So we are back again to the theme of love. How much do you see the beauty in you, the love in you? For when you allow yourselves to remain in situations that do not bring you love but pain, this makes you question, makes you search and always brings you back to the seeking of love, of peace, contentment and happiness.

This is what you seek and search for all of your lives. How much do you value yourselves to want to make this a reality? It can be yours but it requires faith and belief that you are worthy.

Once again we go back to looking at one's self inwardly. The strength you seek is already there inside of you. It is having the belief that it is there waiting to guide you. For when you discover the love that exists in your own heart which is indeed 'You', this love, is such a powerful force, how can it not give you the strength to move through and to remove obstacles in your lives. This is your strength, the strength you seek, love of the self. Sit and listen to the brook, to the stream as the water slowly and quietly trickles towards its destination. Gently, gleaming, it glides passing here and there, over pebbles, over rocks, over branches, over twigs and other obstacles along its path, but nonetheless it does not run any quicker or any faster. It maintains a steady pace, perhaps having to divert its course a little to get around an obstacle, but it does not force itself. It finds a way to manoeuvre around the situation. It follows the path gently where it will eventually merge and be taken along another journey. So be like the brook, be like the stream. Do not hasten through your life's journey. Be patient. It will bring to you happier results.

Patience will bring you peace and the journey will seem more worthwhile because of what you will allow it to offer and present to you along the way. Anything we say to you is always with gentleness. Force will never, and has never brought desired and worthwhile results. Sit and ponder on what ingredients you could add to your life, which you had not given yourself the opportunity of doing before. We assure you, you will not be disappointed. Patience, my friends, is allowing your heart to remain open.

Eternity is not for the chosen few.
It belongs to all of humanity.

FORGIVENESS

Looking to the one who wronged you for forgiveness does not equal the freedom you seek towards ill actions. It may never be realised nor realised to your satisfaction. So my children we say these simple words to you. Look to your own reflection for the forgiveness you seek. Only this will free you from the bondage you have placed yourself in. Only this will allow you to fully participate in life. For to seek gratification from any other source denies you the ability of being a fully committed participant, forever waiting for 'that' moment to arrive. Remember my children, 'that' moment begins with You!

What is the true meaning of forgiveness? Do you forgive because things are going your way, or do you forgive in order to make your own way clear? Forgiving yourself and those who have wronged or hurt you clears the way for your own path, for your own growth and does not entrap you in the negative energy of resentment.

If the person who has wronged you cannot see their wrongdoing and the consequences this action has had on you or another, then find it in yourself to forgive them and the situation itself, so that you may move forward on your journey. Otherwise you will find yourself walking around with this energy trapped within your body, within your aura, carrying it and dragging it behind you. It will colour whatever thoughts or feelings you may have on anything that comes your way or towards another who comes your way. It will be like an underlying force sitting waiting to strike. This is because this lower energy has not been dissipated or released.

We understand that this may not always be easy to do and achieve depending on the situation, depending on the level of hurt, depending on the severity of the affliction towards yourself or towards those you love. This we clearly see, but we say to you, true forgiveness comes from within yourselves, because only you know what you carry in your heart; only you know the true level of your hurts, of your own wounds. Another would like to believe he does or may even think he does, but do not expect others to fully understand your feelings and thoughts because others are not you. They do not live in you. So take responsibility for your own undoing, for your own outworking in those things that are harbouring your progress in this life, in this world.

Waiting for acknowledgment and forgiveness from those who have wronged and hurt you, may not bring you the peace, answers, or the true understanding you seek and which only you can give to yourself. Again it goes back to the self and looking within. There truly lie your answers.

Do not put the responsibility onto others to understand you. Make this your own task, your own duty. Take part in your own unfolding, for that then gives you the power to place yourself in the very place, in the very circumstances you may wish to be in. Doing otherwise, will find you always blaming others and situations. But blame is only stalling time, only delaying the natural process of nature, which begins with the self.

Search for what you want, search for where you would like to be and then act on it. Cannot you see the beauty in this? It is filled with a tremendous powerful energy of being within your own power, within your own centre. It gives one the feeling of being in charge, of feeling centred, of not being taken for a ride and of being led in places not correct for growth. It may be that a particular path is relevant and correct for another, leading him and guiding him on his journey, but it may not be so for you. Therefore learn your own lessons. Observe and remove the things that are in the way and are hampering and hindering your progress.

Forgiveness encompasses within its warm embrace so many other emotions such as compassion, tolerance and humility towards the self and another. It is the seed that will enable you to see your own reflection and ultimately humanity's, through other eyes so to speak. It is the convergence of preconceived thoughts, which were the tools to your own misery, for your own isolation. Forgiveness ultimately leads to love. It is the Golden Chalice standing before you.

For those who have been hurt by ill actions from another, ill actions that you could not possibly imagine another human being could inflict on another human being, you may indeed question - How does one transcend this? How does one comprehend this so as to move on? How does one bring forgiveness into the equation? And, how does one move from the pain that seemingly feels as if one is being engulfed? What does one say to those who are hurting at this level, to this depth?

For the above, again we say and remind you to look within your own heart for there you will find your own freedom, your own salvation. It may take some time, this we understand. We do not ask, suggest or recommend that you skim over your feelings without taking full account of what they speak to you and represent for you. But what we do ask is that, within your own time frame, you firstly forgive yourself, for the pain you have put yourself through. Above all, do not make yourself wrong for the emotions, for the feelings you may have carried or still carry. For indeed your emotions are your own and do not belong to another, so acknowledge and honour them you must.

We then ask, you look within your heart and ask yourself what you could possibly achieve by holding onto those emotions, which are eating you away; eating your very soul. What are these bringing you? Where are they leading you? What is it destroying in your life? What damage is being woven? In what way is this damage running rampant in your life, for if you look deep enough and are honest with yourself, you will see the destructive force it is having, the destructive force it is weaving.

For a child speaks of its true wishes and desires,
so my friends we ask that you honour yourself
the same way.

What of your own soul? What are you doing to yourself? Are you deserving of this pain, of this hurt? Are you deserving of these emotions destroying you? Do you wish to be torn away, piece by piece until you feel like the inside of you is rotting?

Ask yourself all of these questions and there you will find your answer. How much are you hurting those you love and who love you, and who patiently wait by your side trying to understand you? What happens to your other relationships? What of them? What is it creating in your present moment? We cannot tell you what to do. This you must decide for yourself, but we can guide you on why a particular course of action may not be the best, may not be appropriate.

The choice is ultimately yours. Then it is your own decision, for indeed with other lessons, other experiences you will be learning and having, you always learn something. From any experience you may choose to put yourself in, our support is always there to help you turn the corner, to help you make a difference in your life, in your world. Do not look at and place importance on how long you may have trapped yourself in a particular situation - this matters not. What does matter is your present intention. This is what changes anything. This is what brings results which leads to a better tomorrow.

Make a firm intent, a firm decision, a firm commitment on what you wish to do, what you wish to have, which course of action you wish to take, and then act on it. Let that bring you the results. You can always change anything at any moment in your life. There is not, as you may believe, a 'right' moment. Any moment is right. You can walk away and turn away from any situation that you feel is not to your liking and for your highest good. It might have been, once upon a time, but now it no longer brings you satisfaction. Look within yourself and ask, what is it you seek? Ask whether your new decision is for your highest good.

Be responsible and then act on it. Forgiveness begins with the self. Forgiveness is the broom that sweeps clean.

SURRENDER
DETACHMENT

The universe works in mysterious ways at times leaving us perplexed and wondering as to where our next step will lead us. But through this wonderment we realise only too well that surrender we must if we are to work in unison. So in this moment of wisdom, we operate from our true source and silently observe the revelations that each step brings.

How much do you truly surrender to the Heavenly Father, to the Universe, your thoughts and your emotions? How much do you hold on to them and encapsulate them within their own square box? Surrender, we say to you is giving and placing all of your cares, all of your worries to the God force, to the universe for us to partake in, for us to invoke our goodness upon whatever troubles, whatever cares and worries you may have at this present moment in your lives.

We say to you indeed partake in the unfoldment of your own life, but then place the rest in our hands, in God's hands. True surrendering is allowing the universe to work with you. It is not working alone. It is giving to us so that we may shed light on whatever situation may be troubling you in order that you may see other possibilities. Surrendering is helping you see much clearly and deeply into a problem or situation.

For when you allow our guidance to be shared, to filter through, then you see with your soul. This is totally different from seeing with a heart, which is very often closed, and with a head that holds and carries much matter. At times this is too clogged up and overloaded and you then find yourselves unable to see things from a clear perspective because there is not much room, if any at all, for anything new to be entertained, to be given, to be received. It is allowing the natural process to guide you.

This is the true meaning of surrendering. It is not clutching on to your troubles, on to your cares ever so tightly, for nothing can be released when things are held in such a fashion. Because all is encased within your own energy, which is often disguised with fear, anxiety, anguish, pain and so forth. My children, you hold on to your emotions, on to your thoughts so how can you expect yourselves to feel free. It is as if you were hunched over with your arms wrapped around them, protecting them, feeding them over and over, but that traps all energies and does not allow them to filter to the ether, to the cosmos and bring back to you whatever you were wishing for, whatever you intended to happen. They were constantly locked within your embrace.

Anything kept in captivity cannot grow to its full potential, cannot feel total freedom. It is kept alive and survives but in a restricted form. All of these energies cannot transform any situation, cannot shed any light and as a result you cannot help yourself walk towards a better outcome. Train your thoughts; train your mind to let go. It requires practice and at times much practice for a mind not used to this discipline but it can be done, it can be achieved.

Many of you believe surrendering means and is equated to losing control over part of yourself and your life, but that is indeed not so. Surrendering means handing over to enable us to partake in the belief of a higher force. It is having enough faith and enough trust in yourself because letting go does not mean you are not in control, but rather that you are placing whatever thoughts, whatever desires, whatever emotions and whatever troubles you may have into the care of those who see, of those who hear your pleas, your requests and of those who understand. For indeed, there is a higher force at play, which is more than willing to partake in your journey with you.

Therefore, surrendering is allowing your energy and our energy to fuse together. Do not try to outwork everything on your own, for you are not alone. Indeed there is a very kind universe awaiting the surrendering of your own heart to it. Speak gently to us of what it is you wish us to help you with, and then leave the rest to us. Have patience because all will be revealed in its proper manifestation, time and place through the right people or situation. Surrendering is also recognising and understanding that when you surrender to the universe, the requests you have placed in its care may not always come back to you exactly the way you would have wished or anticipated, because we may see a better avenue that will indeed help you further on your path, on your journey, which will give you more clues in claiming the things awaiting you in the future. It is remaining open to receive in the way the universe believes is for your highest good. Your best intentions are always in our minds, in our hearts. We wish nothing but the best for you so whatever we return to you is always with the intention of helping you further on your journey.

However, we remind you, the only way this interaction can truly take place is for you to also play your part, which is through an open heart, with trust and faith in us and in yourself that we are indeed together, united and never separate. Doubt and fear will only make you critical and judgmental of what you receive and of your own inner promptings and urges, thus leaving you in a position of being unable to accept any help at all.

Surrendering is removing all negativity from your thoughts, for negativity is a force unto itself blocking anything else in coming to you and entering your lives. Negative energy carries its own weight and is not of the same force as positive energy. They are in discord and cannot work together. They cannot penetrate into each other. Imagine negative energy as a door, which is blocking all goodness in coming to you. It is a door that is shut and you stand behind this door. Instead, place yourself in the Light. Have the courage to stand in front of the door rather than behind it for it is then that we can send to you all of our healing gifts, all of our goodness.

Detachment we say to you is removing yourself from a situation. It is like having a wish within your mind, a goal, working it all out, creating the vision in your mind then removing yourself from it and giving it room to grow and become your reality. For anything to grow it must be given its own space.

Detachment is very similar to surrendering because when you surrender your cares to the universe, in its own way you are also at the same time detaching yourself. For does not surrendering mean giving way, removing yourself. Thus, if you remove yourself from a situation you must also at the same time be in a space where you are detaching yourself because you are no longer tied to it. Surrendering means no longer being attached to anything in particular and once you are able to do this you automatically detach at the same time. The two work in unison, cohesively. It is as if surrendering was on one side of the coin and detachment was on the other side. As you operate in one mode you automatically allow the coin to flip over for the other to come into play. See the two as a finely tuned working partnership. When you detach yourself from any situation you allow the universe to work in its mysterious ways. It knows how to return to you all its goodness to help you on your journey.

Detachment allows better things to come your way if your original intention was not for your highest good. Your mind may think it knows what is best for you but your soul may feel differently, therefore detaching yourself brings better things your way if your soul feels it is appropriate. Furthermore, remaining attached to an emotion, to an idea keeps you within that energy and draws to you the same or similar situations and experiences.

We again remind you not to outwork and do everything on your own, for mankind was not meant or designed to work all alone. This is not the way God designed the universe. God designed help to always be around. God designed support to always be around. Reflect and think of all the help and support that is indeed always around in your life and in your world. So we say to you, gently speak to us in your hearts. No one else needs to hear your pleas, your requests. Speak to us dear friends, play your part and we will play ours - this is a promise, but you understand we cannot make you do this. You must find it in yourself to want to do this for the rewards are indeed great.

Surrender to the Christ Energy.

Surrender your fears to the Light force and watch magic happen.

Give and place these fears in the hands of the universe.

Detach yourself and watch them disappear.

UNITY

*We must always strive to identify our own humanness
with those around us, for to do otherwise is to stand on
separate grounds with the void being the divide.*

Have the fighting spirit of the warrior. Be fearless. Have the strength of heart to walk through your adversities. For this is the only way to move forward and to reach the other side. Show your spirit to the world. This is your world as much as it is anyone's. So do not hide away.

Make your mark; leave your legacy so that your children may cherish it. Our history, our heritage was very important to us. We knew of the importance of imparting wisdom to our children because we understood they were our future. They walked in our footsteps so we were most careful of what we taught them. We wanted to make them proud of their ancestors, of their culture, of their heritage.

So you too, be a proud nation, proud to have walked this way, proud to leave behind your memories. So do not hide away. Show your strength and let this be the guiding force that steers your children well in their future as they walk their own paths; in time also leaving behind their own legacies, and their own memories for their own children. You must strive to be a proud nation. Pride, that comes from the Spirit and is not a pride based on self-destruction. Pride, which binds people together, that harmonises, brings peace and brings beauty. Not a pride that brings darkness to the soul, to the heart; and darkens the very world in which you live in. Live a simple but a proud life.

Living in harmony, living in togetherness and living in unity will carry a nation through. While discord and wars only separate and divide. These do not bring unity. Instead war hardens the Spirit. There is not much in wars, in fighting: it brings disillusionment to the people and to their hearts. It makes them unable to see their life and life itself any differently. We ask that you work in unison because YOU ALL have the same motivating force IN YOUR SOULS - Peace and Love.

Our tribe was not of many, but we knew how to survive in harmony, we aimed for balance. We treasured our surroundings and because of this we showed our respect to Mother Nature. Mother Nature gave us everything. She was our home. We treated her equally as one of us. She was the land on which we lived and from which we ate so how could we not show her respect. She was owed that much from us.

We only took what we needed and what was necessary for our survival. We never took more than our fair share for we knew we had to live another day. We knew if we abused of her she would not show respect for us. We had to work in unison with her. She taught us unity, respect, beauty. She showed us and shared with us the simple things in life. We were happy and we were contended. So look for the simple things in your own life and be contended. This we say to you, this we pass to you, this we share with you from one heritage to the next.

It matters not what tribe, what nation you come from for the basic rules are the same. Respect Mother Nature. Thank her for what she bestows upon you and what she shares with you. Treat her well and she will treat you with the respect you deserve. Do not awaken the angry spirit in her. Do not hurt her for she will show her vengeful side, not because she does not care for you, but because she is hurting. Just as you let one another know when you are hurting. It is the same principle. It is energy in motion.

*Pedestals are merely illusional and never intended or
designed in bringing people together.*

My people and I have learnt much from being in touch with nature, with all living things. Mother Nature taught us many things. She taught us how to survive in harmony with her. She taught us how to communicate with her. We placed honour very highly - honour of all living things, honour of the self and those amongst us. We knew we were all inter-related, that we co-existed. Therefore, do not be ignorant as to believe yourselves to be separate. You may live in houses removed from the land, but you still depend on Mother Nature to provide for your nourishment in the food you eat, to quench your thirst, from her rivers and dams, and the protection from the heat, which her trees give you.

So, remember, no matter where you are, what mansion you may live in, whatever riches you may have accumulated, remember Mother Nature for what she gives to you daily. For without her, your riches would mean nothing; and your own life you could not even sustain. For these reasons care for her, show your respect and give thanks in the silence of your mind for what she bestows upon you everyday. Give to her a prayer of thanks. Without the seasons you would be nothing and you would have nothing to eat or drink so work together. It is harmony at its best when co-operation is put in place.

Children - teach your children well. Steer them with love. Be firm, be disciplined for this is how they learn; not with harshness but with a guiding force that speaks of gentleness for you are helping to build their character, and you are helping shape their future. They look to you for guidance. They look to you for discipline, for whom else do they have but their elders to steer them, to guide them! Work with them and do not be separate from them. Bind them into your harmony, into your energy and let them then shape their own world, but it would have been firmly based, it would have been firmly rooted and, it would have been well fed. They do not ask that you have all the answers. Learn from your children. Allow yourselves to learn from them as well.

This is how you bind yourselves to each other's energies, two individuals creating one force, working in unison and working in harmony. Children should not be separate because they are younger, and elders on one side because they are older. Each has its rightful place and is there for a reason, there for a purpose. So invite them into your world and allow yourselves to be invited into theirs. Learn from each other. For a future generation to exist there must be children.

What type of future generation do you wish to have and do you aspire for? Question yourselves on this deeply, for it will leave its mark in whatever shape or form. Teach your children compassion, teach them humility, and teach them hope. Teach them of the Spirit; teach them of their true source and of their true origin. Teach them of their strength of character, but remember that you must also be willing to display your own.

Elders, we ask that you also treat your elders with respect. They have lived their time, they have lived their dues. Let them learn from the lessons of life without holding onto remorse, onto regret. If they have learnt and then have shown a different face to the world in their own time, let that speak for itself and find it in your own heart to forgive. For you do not yet know all the lessons awaiting you, or what roads you will still travel. For you see, allowing your elders, and giving them the opportunity to show a different face to the world, gives you the same opportunity should the need arise, should the opportunity present itself. So as we have spoken earlier, about looking at another within yourselves, this you can then understand how true it must be. Let them find his or her, own path. Give them a helping hand but do not bind yourselves to their experiences, for that renders you unable to move along your own journey, along your own path.

Do not judge, for whatever you do to your brother and sister you also do to yourselves. We all have made our mistakes, have learnt our lessons.

Therefore we must give each other and ourselves the opportunity to move beyond and to rise above these. How can the soul move, how can the soul grow and progress if it is constantly reminded of where it has just been? Speak of your hurts if you must, then release them and let them wash away; let them disappear in their rightful place. Do not harbour them. Do not rehash, for that only brings and breeds disharmony. Do not sacrifice your own individuality but by the same token do not create a division between yourself and another. You must find a way to rise above your hurts, above your differences, and the only way to do this is to look inside yourselves where the answers await you. It is there; you will be guided on how to do this for your soul will speak to you.

So God created little children to remind us of our own innocence and sense of free spirit.

Blessed is he who remains open to the wisdom and teachings a child's inner beauty can impart for a fool is he who believes older is always wiser.

Love your children for who they are. Loving them or approving of them only when they meet your expectations becomes conditional rather than unconditional love.

Love them for their sadness. Love them for their pain. Love them for their dislikes. Love them for their fears and for their indifferences. Let them know they are valued in those times as much as you value their laughter, their kindness and gentleness. Above all, do not ridicule.

Let your children know that all feelings and emotions are treated equally. There is no right or wrong, only experiences belonging to the school of life.

Do not protect or covert children too tightly for this will dwarf their ability towards their own understanding of the self and towards their fellow beings. How can one be compassionate, forgiving and tolerant towards another if this cannot be mirrored within?

In order to appreciate our children we must firstly appreciate ourselves. Seeking self-respect from our children is not earned by dictating or imposing. It is earned by one's action towards the self and emanated by example. For what one doesn't possess one cannot give. But it can be cultivated, nurtured and given room to grow.

Let us learn together. Let us dream together. There lies your eternal link. There can you each flower and blossom radiating your own beauty. Let us each speak our Truth.

For though we may be the parent, Must we always be the teacher?

Family, Unison, Unity - Togetherness

Be like a family to one another for indeed you are like a big family in this world for you are all linked. You are God's family in search of your way home.

Serenity, Peace: The way of the warrior in search of himself

The true warrior never gives up, never surrenders himself unto himself until he knows that 'he knows'; until he has found and discovered the Truth. He is always in search of his true mission, of his purpose, of his destiny, how to strive for it and how to reach for it. The warrior knows he is not alone. He knows and sees there are others just like him and it is for this reason he does not destroy as he searches for his quest, but rather shows respect to his fellow warriors along the journey.

He knows what his mission is about, what it stands for. He is in search of his own victory and he knows that no one else can claim it. He must claim what is rightfully his. The true warrior rides like the wind - fearless with his heart, with his Spirit opened to the heavens. He knows he cannot discover all of this alone. He knows that there are higher forces at play and that both are never separate, always united. The warrior guides others behind him and acknowledges those before him. There is no division. So it is we remind you once again of unity. We speak of unity because we know it brings results.

Be proud of Who You Are. Be proud of what you have, people of the world. To want too much, renders you unable to appreciate the things you have in the present moment and keeps you on the sidelines of life itself. Place yourself in the midst of life, participate, observe and interact for then will your cup always be brimming over. Open your heart and together let us walk the journey.

And so we stand before you all, United. All embraced within each other's energy and companionship. We stand here before you, guiding you and reminding you of the simplicities of life. We ask that you look for the simplicities in your own lives and towards life itself. We also ask that you stop and reflect every once in a while in order that you may regroup if need be, before you find yourselves too far removed, too far on a path which is not leading you towards your way home. We stand here sharing our loving presence with you. Take our love within your own hearts, within your own lives and allow it to work its own manifestations.

So dear friends, it has indeed been a pleasure to have this dialogue with you. It has indeed been an honour and a pleasure to partake in your company; to share with you our words of wisdom, our words of truth, that they may help you on your path and journey. Know that love is always at the forefront of anything you wish to do and undertake.

For love will be the compass, which will lead you to your home and keep you on the right roads; so, whichever direction you travel let love guide you. Place it before you begin any journey, any venture.

L for North, **O** for East, **V** for South and **E** for West.
So you can see, it spears in all directions!

L

E   O

V

We send you our blessings of most high.
We watch over you all.
We wish you well. We are always here for you.
We love you all. God Bless.

Amen. White Feather

The 'I' is 'Us' for we are all one and the same.

There is magic in your heart.

There are enough stars for everyone.

www.ingramcontent.com/pod-product-compliance
Lightning Source LLC
Chambersburg PA
CBHW051831040426
42447CB00006B/481